VERSES
WITH
PEPPER

(ALL ABOUT LOVE)

CHORAL PEPPER

For my daughter-in-law
Emily Lowe,
With love and gratitude

Text and illustrations by Choral Pepper

To order additional copies of this book, contact:
Xlibris
1-888-795-4274
www.Xlibris.com
Orders@Xlibris.com

Book Designer: Rick Contreras
Art Director: Mike Nardone

ISBN: 978-1-4010-5992-7 (sc)

Print information available on the last page

Rev. date: 06/23/2020

☙ CONTENTS ❧

ALL ABOUT LOVE

Hearts and flowers,
the icons of romance.
Laughter and tears,
the eternal dance.

Break up and make-up.
Music and wine.
Feed the fire.
Make love sublime.

For love never runs smooth,
It's an up and down track.
It's cry and then soothe,
Leave and come back.

But in the end,
if you don't drop out,
you finally learn
what love's all about.

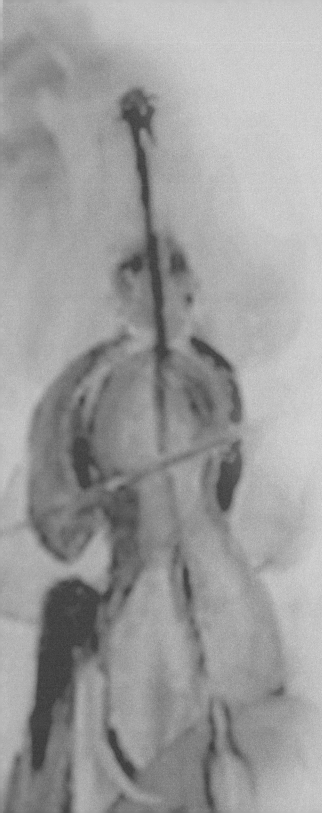

THE INTERLUDE

The best mood
for an interlude
is a romantic one,
If you're twenty-one
and free to wine,
with no deadline.

So let music play
in a dim cabaret
and don't react,
if the deck is stacked
when a stranger appears
and perseveres.

It may be Fate
introducing a mate
to shear like a knife
the dull chords of your life,
and bait your hook
for a new outlook.

A COCK
TO CROW ABOUT

When we first met,
you were at your best.
Needless to say,
I was quite impressed.

I was wowed by your clout
and worldly view.
You were heady fare
For a young parvenu.

But as Time passes along
and you became old shoe,
you still come on strong,
you old Cock-a-Doodle-Do.

THE SNARE

Some come bearing gifts
Others come begging gifts;
Whichever it is
Beware!
A giver demands toll,
A taker extracts dole.
It's a nightmare!

There's a giver and taker
In every affair.
So approach your romance
With *laissez-faire*.
Or else avoid the snare
With Solitaire.

TONIGHT IS THE NIGHT!

Let corks pop.
Let music play.
Tonight is the night
for an ardent entrée
of tender caresses
and romantic toasts,
of eager yesses
by the bedpost.

Seize the moment.
Let's have fun.
Tonight is the night.
It's all-or-none!

WELL-BALANCED

Some guys are handsome,
some are big and strong.
Some make a million,
some are never wrong.

But you, in your modest way,
put them all to shame.
While they flaunt a resumé,
you bask in shy acclaim.

For who else, I ask you,
Can walk a straight line
After two steins of beer
And a jug of red wine?

YOU'RE ONLY AS OLD AS YOU *FEEL*

The little old lady,
so noble and wise,
had inner compulsions,
To her own surprise.

"Should I?" or "Shouldn't I?"
her conscious gasped
as temptation reared itself
into her grasp.

Then "Why not?"
an inner voice called.
"You're as old as you *feel*,
so why be appalled?"

No one was looking.
It was just a quick pinch.
The young man was busy,
with ne'er a flinch.

But the little old lady,
so young and gay,
grandly sailed on.
She'd had a nice day!

THEY NEVER FORGET...

Lovers rotate like a revolving door.
Some come rich, others poor.
Some we recall like a well-worn doll.
Others last as long as the ball.

But there is one a man never forgets,
One who flamed like hot briquettes,
Then disappeared with the game still in play.
They never forget the one that got away.

BUS STOP

When black clouds burst
over the bus stop,
neither stranger knew
the power of a raindrop.

She shared her umbrella.
He moved in close.
It was a subtle start
for a metamorphose.

He didn't foresee
his single life at stake.
She didn't endeavor
to put on the brake.

Wouldn't you know,
it led straight to bed?
By sharing her umbrella,
she became a newlywed.

THE DIVORCE

Come celebrate
my new estate.
I dumped the louse
and got the house.
He can lay his harem
I won't scare 'em.

It was a pitiful spot
To have and have not.
But I won in the end,
so please attend
my initiation
into single taxation.

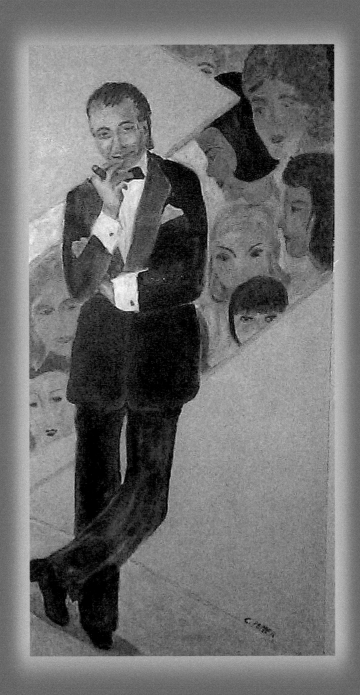

UNBOUND

Unbound am I
aloft and free.
My sails burst with life
o'er land and sea.
I'm joy unbound,
with love all around.
How great to be me
And so blessedly free!

ONCE UPON
A DREAM

Once upon a dream
there appeared
astride a moonbeam
a kindly wizard
who made a vow
to endow
my fondest wish
with one swish
of his magic wand.
What could I respond?

My children were safe.
My love secure.
A dove cooed above
like a troubadour.
Flowers blossomed
at my feet.
My life as it was
was quite complete.

The important things
I already have,
a life like wellsprings
of happiness.
So take my joy
and spread it afar.
That is my wish
on every star.

WHO'S THE TOP BANANA NOW?

You were the top banana,
The CEO,
The honcho in charge
From the very get-go.

I bowed to your will.
I never said "no."
You kept me safely at bay
Like in an escrow.

Until the day
I became your wife.
Things changed then.
It was a whole new life.

Now decisions are mine.
I decide right from wrong
I rule my realm
From a velvet chaise-longue.

In the office you reign
But at home I'm the boss
My former behavior
For a wife would be dross.

Now you bow to my will,
And always say "yes."
Any woman can do it
If she uses finesse.

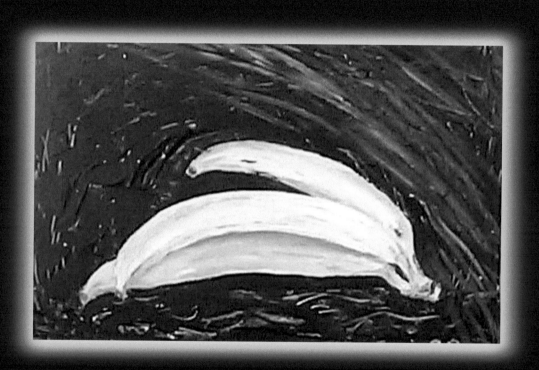

IS *THIS* ALL THERE IS?

She wore a veil,
He wore a tux.
Their march down the aisle
Was *trés deluxe.*

Then TV set in
and what a din!
Day and night,
a game or fight.

She made it clear,
as he guzzled beer,
that she wanted to yack,
but he hit the sack.

Is *this* all there is?
Is the world *all* his?
A common cry
'twixt girl and guy.

RAINY DAYS

It rained when we met.
It rained when we said goodbye.
Then you turned your back
And left me to cry.

But I have been here before.
I know you'll be back.
You think love's a swinging door.
This time, it's a cul-de-sac.

I've had my last heartburn.
I'll recover very well.
There will be no return
When you ring my doorbell.

One lesson I've learned,
broken hearts always mend.
We have once to be burned
To reap that dividend.

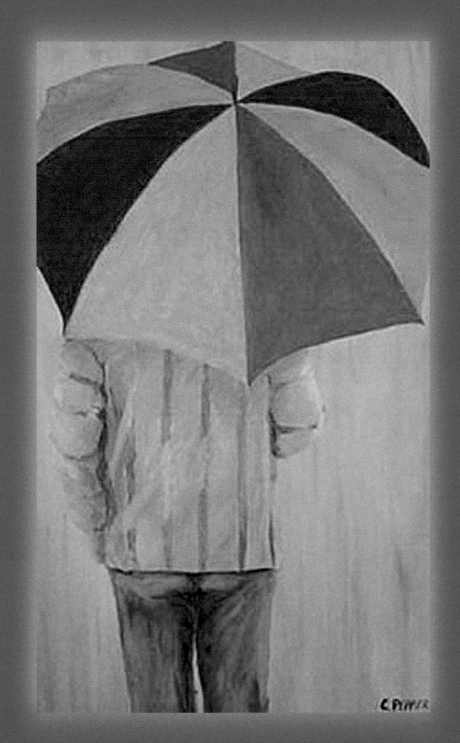

SUPERIORITY

She struts down the street.
Men gather to stare.
They want to stop her,
But do they dare?

Haughty and chic,
she looks straight ahead,
aware their technique
leads straight to bed.

This girl is no hussy.
Fastidious and fussy,
she knows how to freeze
a suggestion of sleaze.

So shape up, lad
and be mighty glad
that some girls exist
who willfully insist
upon a candidate
with a wedding date.

RIPTIDE

The sun burned bright,
The water turned blue.
I got caught in a riptide
And parted from you.

I fought to stay afloat,
To get back to shore.
I never imagined
A better Fate lay in store.

Sometimes it takes
A cataclysmic upset
To force new colors
On Life's palette.

My yesterdays are valuable
For what they taught.
If happiness depends upon another
We have nothing but naught.

I know that truth now.
I am independent and free.
If I can't love myself,
Who should bother to love me?

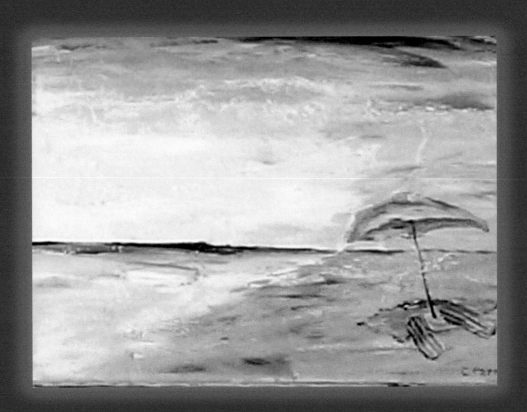

THE INVITATION

Come dine with me.
The best is yet to be.
No need to dress, black tie *et al*,
I'll wear my pearls.
We'll have a ball.
What lies ahead,
besides getting fed?
It's a night for surprises,
to see what rises!

ODE TO AN EX-LOVER

Lady Chatterley's lover
made love under cover.
He knew his game.
Hers was the same.

For the trysts they shared
with everything bared,
they paid a price.
But wasn't it nice
to have a lark,
and ignite the spark
before it burned out
And they both grew stout?

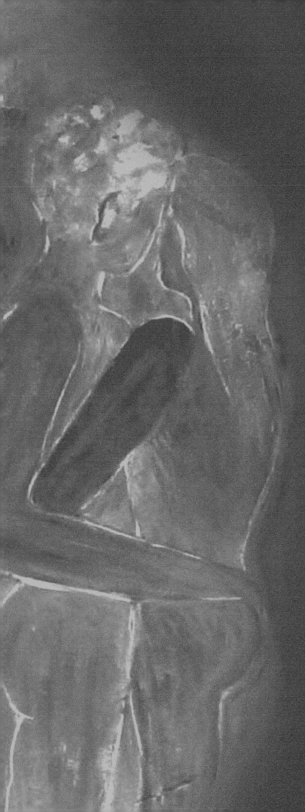

THROUGH
THE KEYHOLE

Now let's be explicit
About love illicit.
What goes on in privy
without your skivvy
can be gloriously hot
if you're not caught.

But if the keyhole is rigged
with some thingamajig
and your secret is out
for the world to shout,
you pay for your folly.
And the trial ain't jolly.

Some say what they pay
For the right to stray
is worth the cost
whatever is lost.
So decide if it's risky
before you get frisky.

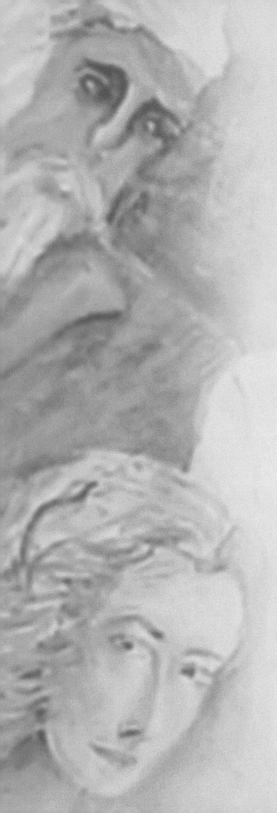

WHODUNNIT?

Á LA AGATHA CHRISTIE

Was it the gardener
who tended the grounds?
Or the man-of-the-cloth
making his rounds?
The victim's brother?
A neighboring squire?
Did they have motives
for murder so dire?

Not the grieving widow
with the red hair,
unless someone recalled
her flagrant affair.
The prime suspect,
they all agreed,
 was the lady's maid,
driven by greed.

Then onto the scene
came the pipe-smoking sleuth
to tie up loose ends
and reveal the truth.
"Who dunnit?" he asked.
"Not I," they each said.
"You may be right,
but the victim is dead."

So he interviewed each
of the parties suspected
and finally proved
'twas the one least expected!

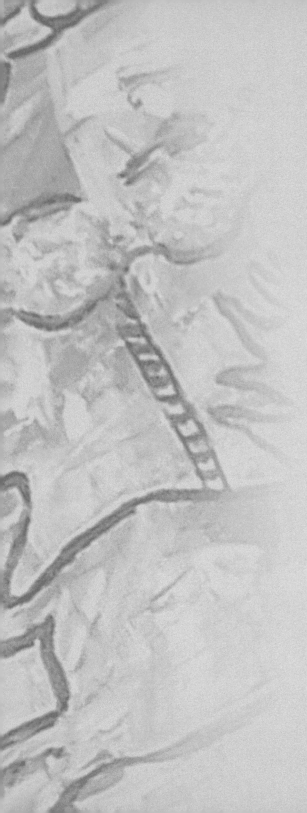

LOVE IS A
CAROUSEL

Up and down,
around and around.
The carousel of love
spins on, unbound.
The gold ring tempts
at every turn,
but my steed moves too fast
and forever I yearn
for a calliope song
keyed to my speed
so I can seize the ring,
and with love, succeed.

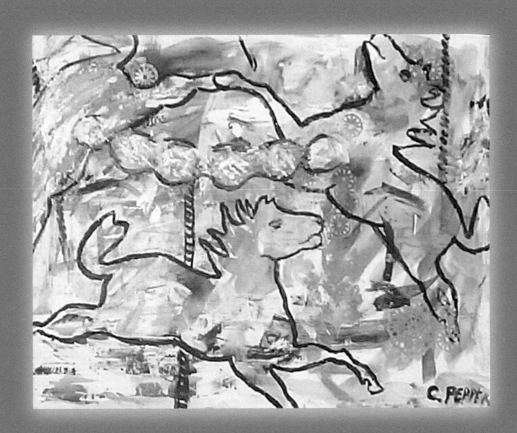

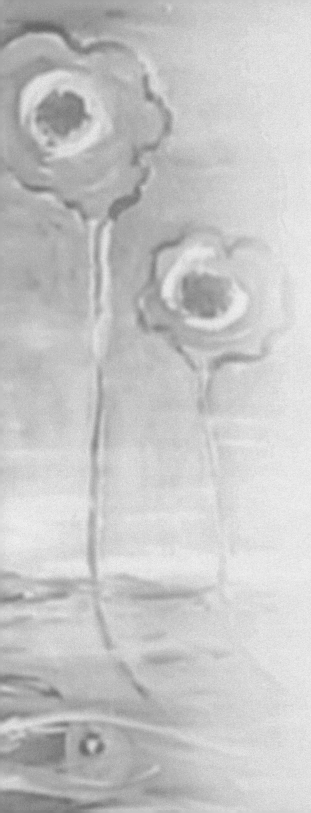

FIFTEEN MINUTES OF FAME

She was in the right place
At the right time
to fleetingly embrace
her moment sublime.

It came and then went
like a flickering flame.
Celebrity today.
Tomorrow, no name.

But o'er land and sea
Once her face spread.
For that fifteen minutes,
the whole world read
of where she was
for her Moment of Fame,
at the right time
to reap the acclaim.

SOUL MATE

I waited for my soul mate,
certain he would come along.
I waited and waited and waited,
composing a tender love song
to express my longing for him,
this man so handsome and strong.

But years slid by
And he never appeared,
although others passed by,
either stupid or weird.
So I finally gave up
and got a job,
quit dreaming futile dreams
and being a snob.

Then along he came,
neither princely nor strong,
but a very wise man
and, he loved my song!

Printed in the United States
By Bookmasters